Our Neighbourhood Houses

COLOURED VERSION

CHILDREN SAVING OUR PLANET SERIES

CAROL SUTTERS

Illustrated by William Fong

AuthorHouse™ UK
1663 Liberty Drive
Bloomington, IN 47403 USA
www.authorhouse.co.uk
UK TFN: 0800 0148641 (Toll Free inside the UK)
UK Local: 02036 956322 (+44 20 3695 6322 from outside the UK)

Because of the dynamic nature of the Internet, any web addresses or links contained in this book may have changed since publication and may no longer be valid. The views expressed in this work are solely those of the author and do not necessarily reflect the views of the publisher, and the publisher hereby disclaims any responsibility for them.

Any people depicted in stock imagery provided by Getty Images are models, and such images are being used for illustrative purposes only.
Certain stock imagery © Getty Images.

This book is printed on acid-free paper.

ISBN: 978-1-6655-8787-7 (sc)
ISBN: 978-1-6655-8788-4 (e)

Library of Congress Control Number: 2021907242

Print information available on the last page.

Published by AuthorHouse 04/12/2021

authorHOUSE®

Tom and Kate and Mum now walk to school every day.

On the way they pass lots of houses which have blocks on the roof.

"*What is the block on that roof?*", asks Kate.

"*That is a solar panel*", says Mum.

"It is all part of us going green and reducing our carbon emissions. Do you remember the solar farms we saw on the way to the seaside when we went on holiday?"

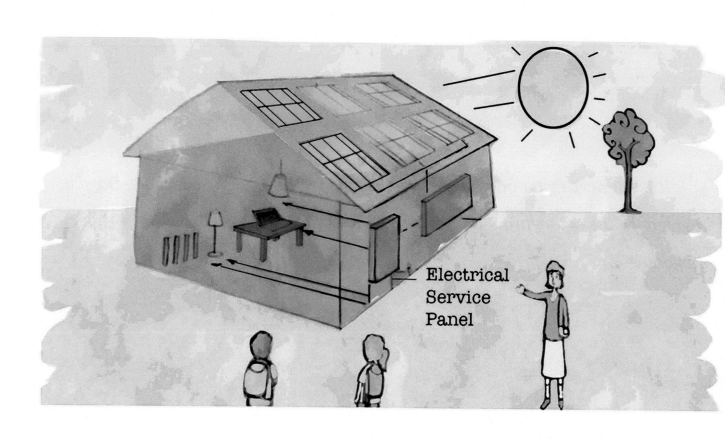

Electrical
Service
Panel

"The solar panel traps energy from the sun's rays. The solar panel transfers the sun's energy into pipes and wires in the rods which heat the water in the house. This keeps it warm inside in winter. The solar panels can also generate electricity."

"The family can send extra electricity which they do not use to the electricity power station so that other families can buy it and use it."

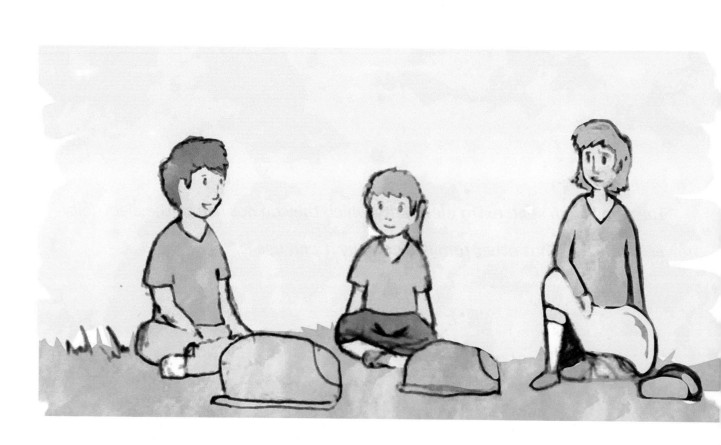

"Why is that called going green?", says Tom.

"It means we did not have to burn coal, oil or wood to heat the house or water. This means we do not use up sources of coal or oil which occur naturally in our earth."

"In this way we preserve these useful fossil fuels for others to use. We also preserve trees by not burning wood. By not burning these we produce less toxic gases such as carbon dioxide which is made by burning oil, gas and wood."

"This will help to preserve planet earth for our grandchildren to enjoy", says Mum.

"There are lots of houses with solar panels", says Kate.

"Yes", says Mum. "Nowadays there are less chimneys on rooves for coal fires in the lounge and more solar panels on rooves. We try to discourage people from having open coal or wood fires in their houses for heating."

"I think solar panels on rooves are very clever", says Kate. *"I hope many more houses get them."*

Sun rays are important for solar panels to work.

"Solar energy helps us to live healthier lives", says Mum, "and it helps us use natural energy from sunlight. This is called renewable energy which means it will never run out or be in short supply, as will happen with fossil fuels. Solar power will continue as long as the sun keeps shining."

"Generating solar energy is an important new source of work for many people. As we reduce coal fired power stations those people working there with fossil fuels can seek jobs in renewable energy companies as an alternative."

What did we learn today? (tick the box if you understood and agree)

☐ Solar panels trap energy from the sun.

☐ The energy can be used to heat water and generate electricity.

☐ This is called renewable energy.

☐ If we use solar energy we avoid burning fossil fuels which damage animals

and plants on our planet.

Find out about Tom and Kate's neighbourhood roads in book 6.

Children Saving our Planet Series

Books

1. **Tom and Kate Go to Westminster CHILDREN'S REVOLT**

2. **Kate and Tom Learn About Fossil Fuels**

3. **Tom and Kate Chose Green Carbon**

4. **Tress and Deforestation**

5. **Our Neighbourhood Houses**

6. **Our Neighbourhood Roads**

7. **Shopping at the Farm Shop**

8. **Travelling to a Holiday by the Sea**

9. **Picnic at the Seaside on Holiday**

These series of simple books explain the landmark importance of Children's participation in the Extinction rebellion protest. Children actively want to encourage and support adults to urgently tackle both the Climate and the Biodiversity emergencies. The booklets enable children at an early age to understand some of the scientific principles that are affecting the destruction of the planet. If global political and economic systems fail to address the climate emergency, the responsibility will rest upon children to save the Planet for themselves.

This series is dedicated to

Theodore, Aria and Ophelia